Fro Bone to Blossom

s by Eileen Casey
Pen and Drawings by Emma Barone

Introduction From Bone to Blossom
Eileen Casey and Emma Barone

A long time ago they told us stories so we could learn how to become people. Hand in hand with that tradition came the practise of creating images by which to explore and describe experience. Collected here, the recent work of Emma Barone and Eileen Casey, fuse two lines of tradition. In this shared space, word and image work off one another; Barone's striking images of Coastal Trees complement Casey's engaging poems, while Casey's poems expand the rooted territory of Barone's images; the two media making for a deeper interpretation of the title landscape, *From Bone to Blossom*.

Directly Barone's images pull us into a realm of prevailing wind, struggle against the elements: a full sense of what *Bone* might mean. Strong black lines sweep through the trees, their chastened branches scrape at the atmosphere around them, and are echoed in Casey's lines where she tells us what she touches is 'a woman with sharp corners/daggers at shoulder blades, knives in her eyes/scratching the sky with broken fingernails'. First and foremost these images and poems relate to us the matter of *Bone*, how it is to 'steer under/ gull's lonely sough' and ride out the 'weathers of the heart'.

Casey's poetry is deeply rooted in the matter of being human and how it is for our Bone selves to live in the prevailing wind of ordinary life with its 'bitter streets that taste of dust'. She is generous with the moods and 'weathers' of her own life, but she also possesses an empathetic eye that observes and relates other people's stories. Casey's human portraits are all in relationship with one another, underscoring our mutuality and common experience, in the same way that Barone's trees are united by their prevailing wind and linked by their conspicuous *Bone* trunks.

The wind that blows through Casey's poems knows our lives can be 'blushed by circumstance', that it's possible to be 'out on a limb' and have the gods 'deal an extra blow'. She relates a debilitated man unable to climb stairs and describes the injustice of two old ladies who experience 'breaking glass, threats' and having to flee, 'barefoot through brambles'. She tells of being 'magnified by our isolation' and 'diminished', the poet aware that sometimes all we're left with is 'a rustling thirst/snagged on a blackthorn tree'. Repeatedly Casey shows us our vulnerability within single deft lines: the 'little left' in her 'dreaming pouch', describing perfectly the bereft, *Bone*-like existence the gale can reduce us to.

As Barone's images mount up we see beyond wind, beyond *Bone*; the dominant, seemingly challenged trunks also express a quality of endurance. We perceive that nothing will disfigure these boles, mar their thick branches, or harm their resistant mangrove-like roots. The wind persists and Barone's strong black branches articulate a fortitude that is echoed in Casey's lines:

> We draw back our bow as evenings shorten into winter
> twisting baroque branches around our empty spaces.

Barone asks us to look again at what *Bone* might also contain, just as Casey leads us to glimmers of redemption within struggle. For Casey ordinariness has within it a particular, almost elegant music that the poet hears and lovingly recreates, 'A blackbird's note drips down the eaves/he's waited until afternoon'. She finds a hedgehog, 'barely noticeable on the bristly texture of our mat', but Casey does notice, persistently pointing out small marvels within the quotidian world. In poems ripe with detail and inherent with courage, she charts the building of a house, day by day, the passage from shed to washing line. This matter of our life, 'Shoulder to wheel, nose to grindstone' is the essential condition of the world, 'swallows too follow nature's deciduous ways/build their nests from spit and clay'.

But if the world around her is 'tall and straight', its undersides are also 'downy'. In Casey's *Bone*, in the state of endurance she witnesses, there is a kind of grace, 'green glimpses seek us out'. Though climbing offers 'laboured breaths', they 'stream out white ribbons' the poet binds around her 'dreaming leaves'. Beds may be for 'our rising' but they are also for the 'buck of passion', 'warmth' and 'love'. Within the 'weather' of ordinary life Casey sees a mystic wealth; she suffuses endurance with 'rituals'. A porch light exists not for practical purpose, but to give solace to 'the wanderer'. We have 'The Miracle of Bees', and descriptions of 'alchemy'. For the poet 'doorways to mystical worlds' are 'natural as pauses/in conversations'. Right down in the hardship of Bone, Casey finds *Blossom*.

Each of Barone's trees *Blossom*. They articulate a lively, endlessly imaginative, expression of fulfilment. They have a playful sense of humour and yet inhabit an entirely serious space. Despite, or even because of, the wind, they unfurl unique blooms, masses of florets; marine, kelp-like corolla; earthy, female trumpets; art deco squares. They flower with delicate precision, each one individual, exact, yet flowing according to its own essential nature. Casey suggests 'we find green shoots'. Barone discovers them and amplifies them into stylistic, elegant designs. In her poem 'Timber', Casey tells us

3

'flamboyance blossoms on the blackthorn tree', echoing and expressively describing Barone's images.

Casey *Blossoms* in similarly imaginative and redolent ways. Her poems chart the full range of joy. We experience the miracle of birth, honour long-lasting love in her beautiful poem 'Soot', and repeatedly take strength from the way she eulogises nature, praising its grand gestures and minute deeds. For Casey the territory of Blossom is intimately connected with the space of dreaming, the potential to 'dream' and recreate the world anew. The poem 'Taken with my Shutter-Box eye' opens with the bold statement: 'Butterflies for transformation' and highlights Casey's interest in change, redirection and metamorphosis, liberating the reader into their own creative dreamings. Seduced by the delights of Casey's 'mulberry' dreaming, we enter wholeheartedly into celebration of her 'magenta coming of age'.

It is interesting to see how both artists use colour within their work. Often colour enters the pen and ink drawings with the same discretion that Casey sews it into her poems. Both artists know the value in holding back. Sometimes Casey offers us shy glimpses, a prick of blood on a finger, a charcoal smudge, lemon ice-cream. Then, like Barone's trees, she gives us pages of black and white; we are absorbed in mood and interior contemplation. We turn the page and unexpectedly Casey gives us the whole rainbow. She stands in the paint shop deriding magnolia; requiring 'vermillion', 'atomic orange', 'Mediterranean blue'. Barone takes these colours, wraps them around her *Blossoms* and the trees deepen, their *Bone* becoming more luminous.

Yet the heart of this book is much more than personal journey, Casey's poems also voice a social conscience and environmental concern that resonates through, and informs all, the other pieces collected here. There are important poems in these pages that alert us to the prevailing wind of the future. Oil spills, deforestation, clean water, 'tribal battles for spaces growing fewer', and the increasing need for millions of people to 'wear their home around' their shoulders, bring the 'understory' of our time into a space where its *Bone and Blossom* can no longer be ignored. Expressed here is the gentle voice of female outrage. It is graceful, subtle; full of poetry and alarm. Excellent poems like 'The Earth Replenishes Itself', 'The Texaco Art Competition', and the enduringly powerful 'Woman Wearing her Home around her Shoulders' ring out with a voice that must be heard, paid attention to and acted upon. The book's call for transformation is built on pressing foundations and Casey's is a wise and still voice that we can only trust.

Overall there is a tension held here that concerns itself with the nature of transformation. The title and the title poem *From Bone to Blossom* suggest a journey, from one condition to the other,

> 'there is much to make of the journey, its push
> towards the light—darkness too.
> Without shade, there would be no truths,
> no beauty'

Yet what also comes forward is the sense that the two spaces of *Bone and Blossom*, can simultaneously co-exist. In certain religious traditions the pilgrim is given a spiritual name, a title that describes an aspirant state of grace, or *Blossom*, that the seeker wishes to attain—and yet already, innately possesses. The seeker's journey or 'push towards the light' that Casey articulates, is in fact, like the enduring *Bone* and fulfilled *Blossom* of Barone's trees, present all along: it just needs to be perceived.

The poems range across a wide canvas, we visit Verona, South America, the Tundra, Galway and Ancient Greece, yet the drawings remain in the one place. They repeat and progress in a meditative study. Barone's focus is held within the tensions of wind, root, *Bone*, and *Blossom*. Barone directs us: look, listen, review perspective. The swirling, marine branches of her trees pull us back into the same space, the simultaneous holding of *Bone* and *Blossom*, reminding us that what both artists are defining, are spaces of suffering and endurance, spaces of courage and grace. Meanwhile Casey's poems bring these pen and ink drawings on a global journey; in South America, in Europe, on the Tundra, these same spaces and forces exist. The trees are relocated.

Barone instructs meditation, still awareness of what already is, Casey encourages voyage, movement from darkness to light but she is also aware that both methods of transformation can co-exist: on occasion we may be immersed in darkness and only make a slow progressive journey back to light, at other times we can make a shift of perception and see the *Blossom* that was there all along. What both artists know is that modern popular culture, with its pursuit of happiness, seeks endless *Blossom* and forgets the necessity and power of *Bone*. These artworks remind us how is it to live with a prevailing wind, how to endure and flourish. Both Emma Barone and Eileen Casey know that whatever our spiritual aspirations, we are merely people blown about by external forces. How we meet those forces is what is examined here, for these are narratives of becoming.

Grace Wells

Eileen Casey

Eileen Casey, originally from the Midlands, is based in South Dublin. Her work is widely published in outlets such as *Poetry Ireland, Abridged, Books Ireland, Senior Times, Ireland of The Welcomes, The Chaffin Journal (USA), The Coffee House* (UK),*The Irish Times, The Stony Thursday Book, The Stinging Fly, The Moth, Verbal Arts Journal, The Sunday Tribune, Riposte, The Offaly Anthology, A.I.D.'S West, Crannog, County Lines: A Portrait of a County* (New Island). Twice short listed for a Sunday Tribune Hennessy Award (fiction and poetry), her debut poetry collection *Drinking the Colour Blue* (New Island) was published in 2008. *From Spit and Clay*, a poetry chapbook, won the 2010 Green Book Festival Award, Los Angeles (poetry category).

'Reading Fire, Writing Flame', a solo exhibition awarded by Offaly County Council went on show at Arás An Chontae, Tullamore, 2007. A founder member of Platform One (Rua Red Arts Centre, Tallaght), she is also a member of Thornfield Poets. Recent poetry awards include The Oliver Goldsmith International Poetry Prize, The Hannah Grealy Award and The Black Diamond Poetry Awards. In 2010 she received an Arts Council individual artist bursary and is currently a postgraduate student on the Master of Philosophy (Creative Writing), Trinity College, Dublin.

'*Drinking the Colour Blue* is a substantial debut with moments of surreal beauty'
– *The Irish Times*.

'Seldom do I run into such a capable poet, one whose work is so delicious to read: well written, honest, accurate and compelling'
– Dorothy Sutton, Emerita Foundation Professor of English and Creative Writing, Eastern Kentucky University.

Emma Barone

Emma Barone is a Visual Artist based in Birr, Co. Offaly. She spent many years studying and working in the areas of animation, interior design, graphics and jewellery. She has also worked with stained glass, mosaic, architectural ceramics, visual merchandising and kitchen design. Her work has been featured in several magazines such as *The Irish Arts Review, Senior Times, House and Home, Midland Arts, Midland Tribune* and *The Sunday Independent,* among others. She has enjoyed seven successful solo exhibitions to date, the most recent in The Watergate Gallery, Kilkenny. She has also participated in numerous group exhibitions, including several juried shows all over Ireland. Her works hang in public collections in the Amsterdam World Trade Centre, Offaly County Council Public Offices, Midland Regional Hospital and throughout Ireland, Europe and the United States.

In 2008, a collaboration with writer Eileen Casey resulted in Reading Hieroglyphs in Unexpected Places (Fiery Arrow Press), a publication featuring poetry and shoe images.

'A book of magical shoes/a book of magical poems about shoes. A truly special collaboration between two highly accomplished and creative women' — *The Sunday Independent*

An attractive book with its quirky design and paintings of shoes in bright colours. Barone's paintings are eye-catching and Casey brings in references and imagery that at first may not seem obvious but which set off flights of fancy in the reader's mind' — *Books Ireland*

The Beauty of Shadow

I dip parched hands in its ancient pool. An oarswoman
pushing off from familiar shores turns her back
on tidal days, those ebbs and flows of happiness.

I am no saint. I burn, look to the shadow
cast by oak deepening down, further even
than sins committed before I was born.
I too have added to their store.

I steer under gull's lonely sough, weathers of the heart
forecast by darkening skies. It cools my skin
slips its moist flesh over me,
a prized caul, protection from too much sun.

I bathe my breasts in silky moss and lichen, breezes
brush berries. I drown in rosy midnight.
My feet I leave until the very last, so many miles
walked or ran from the source, like roots
twisted away from yet mapping a way back.

In the shadow of oak, I hear the linnet's song
fed on weed, caterpillars. I see the moon's face,
mirror bright.

Spinlethorns

White fences make good neighbours

I'm painting the fences white, shed too,
white as a gumdrop or a wedding shoe.

When that's done I'll float in a summer palace
canopied by pale-leaved whitebeam trees,
lie on a blanket with my ice coloured cat
eat cake, be cooled by spigots of light.

I'll read about Antarctica while butterflies
ripen like berries, ignore warning telegrams
pipped by a blackbird
three tiers up at least.

I'll be whitening out lawnmowers, chainsaws,
barking feuds, a neighbourhood's graffiti of sound.

Mulberry Silk

Hum

Sometime in the small hours, our fridge breaks down.
You fill the sink for milk carton, exactly quarter full
as if it were a science, not old ways.

Who knows better? You as child burying meat and butter
in damp earth behind your mother's house.
Summer the worst,

rhododendrons circling the lake, the reek of food
going off in the rusted Jacob's tin, lowered
two feet down at least,

under shades of Torc, Mangerton, Tomies Mountain,
three lakes meeting, where, in the middle of the night,
two old ladies fled from breaking glass, threats.

Barefoot through brambles and that cricket sound,
close as could be touched, sending shocks through the tall grass,
fish darting tremors, you, days later, walking the shore,
around you in waves that humming sound.

Sycamore Eyes

The Miracle of Bees

This summer, a flood of bees drench skins of leaves,
a strange music for which I have no name.

I do not fear their ways.

In ancient Greece shipbuilders caulked
joints with wax, waterproofed hulls of vessels
for safe passage across swarming waters;

whether for battle or for pleasure.

Homer wrote of war ships with painted images
sailing into Troy.

Why would I fear to go from shed to washing line
or sit beneath the veins of bending leaves?

These tiny Merlins
possess the alchemy to transform
labour into fragrant wax
I pour across the canvas of my white page
solidifying -
even as it leaves the flame −

the fiery stings of memory.

Picasso Noon

Climbing

These nights
what little's left in my dreaming pouch
dreams a beanstalk soon gone wild.
I climb to where my child must surely be
imprisoned in a giant's keep.

Laboured breaths above cold rooftops
stream out white ribbons I try
to bind around my dreaming leaves;
before mighty footsteps toss and turn
these clouds,

tumble me back to earth.

Silver Apples

Winter Hedgehog

Beyond the margins of our berried fruitfulness
a hedgehog's skin rugs the pavement, brought down
perhaps by fox or badger, more likely speeding car
on rain slicked suburban street. These last two nights

it's poured down, half the country flooded, gardens
mulched, hawthorn leaves and earth clogging drains.

Whatever it was tore out its belly in the small hours
has been and gone, two clenched November moons
sunk into quick-sands of two new dawns.
Vanished too, warm Azores, winds prickling
from its soft bed under our rosy hedgerow,

this spiky urchin to forage a puzzle of a season.

The hedgehog dead outside our gate
might well be the one surprised the year before
curling tight against us in porch light glare,
barely noticeable on the bristly texture of our mat,
who, when pooled again in darkness
licked its tongue the whole length of its body
anointing away the scent of us.

Shawl

The Texaco Art Competition

Splashed on a child's canvas, shades of an Amazon
lost by oil spills. No smoke or charcoal here, no sludge
or vultures circling.
A few miles east of Coca lies the village of San Carlos,
cut through for exploration, farming -
hardly any forest left now.

A young girl with a spear through her stomach
shaped as the sandpapery leaves of the Cecropia
(named for the mythical king of Athens)
stains the forest floor with blood.
Tribal wars battle for spaces growing fewer,
where macaws draw out blue, gold and scarlet plumage
or water runs clear.

A man weeps here. He has become
like a Philo (love) Dendron(tree).
Branches twisted and deformed
as the limbs of his children,
shape towards an understory.

Prickly Spruce

Woman wearing her home around her shoulders

Where you live means 'end of the world'.
A mammoth calf, thousands of years old,
found on this peninsula was one winter young
at time of death – the same age as your baby son.

No treelines shield. Tundra winds unpick
your way of life, loosen stitching on your Yamal home –
a tent made from dried reindeer.
Your husband drank its still warm blood,

coming to you all those months ago
raw flesh in his mouth, smells of slaughter
sown into each crease and crevice of his skin.
Below the mark where steel struck bone,

together at night you lie. Steel slit the reindeer's throat
wide as the opening where your head pokes out.
You gaze upon these rolling miles and it seems
as if your home is wrapped around your shoulders.

You gauge the time to rise like birds, make your way
from north to summer pastures in the south;
waiting for the river Ob to freeze (already late)
while all along Siberia's northwest coast
thousands of barrels are emptying out your world.

Elderberry China

Song Note

That round coin of ice on the rain-barrel finally tips in,
flipping up on one side the same as our silver rimmed mirror.
A blackbird's note drips down the eaves, he's waited
until afternoons most days to come and feast on cold soup,
left-overs strung across our hedgerows
bright as a gypsy's washed out clothes
on days that aren't nomadic.

We too become settled in our weather,
rituals performed when we can't go outside
passing time with making toast and cups of tea
at unlikely moments, going to bed for warmth
or love. When we should be at our desk,
in the car, supermarket, or someplace else
but here, under a circle of glass where we are
magnified by our isolation, or diminished.
Too much small talk.

Yet, water chortles down the chutes again,
green glimpses seek us out, the world
dropping back to where it left us days ago.

Scythe Tree

Cenote

Doorways to mystical worlds, natural as pauses in conversations
stooped or crawled towards or swung down to through mouth and eye.
What can be worse than the lonely fall, a pine tree cone
becoming the grenade of silence?

On root and branch, limb articulates to limb
forming solitary ridges or the antlers of a rutting stag.
A bird's beak is bone yet builds nests in bowl and leaf.

We find green shoots. Postcards through letterboxes
sent back by children flung like seed over whole
continents. Travelling back on heavy inked wings.
We pitchfork the skies, bring home turf-bark,
stacked to make canoes or sturdy ropes,

lobed winged dreaming maps.
Year after year we feel the rush of air, swallows
returning to summer meadows.

Acrobats

My Shutter-box Eye

Butterflies for transformation, peonies for perception.
In swirls of chi energies a phoenix freezes its soaring –
everything stopping for eleven o'clock tea
(it can rid you of bad dreams, strengthen your bones –
even act as an aphrodisiac).
Flocks of evergreen lotus spring from tight buds
an octopus scuttles across an ocean sky. Colour through
the lens of leaf clicks tree millinery, shapes block brim
Buddhas. Placed on Medusa's head I am unable to sleep
a full seven nights after.
Spindlethorns bewitch a coalmine sky,
crack the riggings. Ice breaks.

I took the outline of Wisdom too and a certain kind of truth,
crystalline, sharp as a dragon's tooth.
In these stills
encampments pitch their tents
hang out washing on a rowan tree's blessing.

Hornbeam Wheel

Let us build this house

where sycamore seahorses ride out to touch the sky
with wood ox-strong, its creamy skin luminous in dusk
porch light for the wanderer.

Let us build brick upon brick, leaf upon leaf,
a violin winging seeds of our music far and wide
scattering with our children to the four corners.

This timber's song is sharp enough to spear
through history. Maple wood migrated here,
first stood firm east to the Caucasus, north to Paris.

We draw back our bow as evenings shorten into winter
twisting baroque branches around our empty hearths.

Electric Storm

The Earth Replenishes Itself

'The art of dreaming is the art of living. Everything we say and do is an
expression of the force of life. The creation is ongoing. It is endless.
It is happening in every moment' –
Don Miguel Ruiz

It would be good to think Polar Bears safe, rainforests growing back
like haircuts or clipped nails, carbon footprints barely traceable
all desecrations of the day - sprays, fumes, spills and spoils
lured back into nurturing space.

A skier at the Chacaltya Ski Resort in Bolivia
finishes on foot, snow giving way to sand and rock.
It would be good to think while we are sleeping
snow falls thick and fast and sticks in that place
sunlight warming where it should -
new moons of March and April lit by earthshine.
Mangrove swamps, lush, Madagascar restored.

A medicine man passes down such wisdom
while we are sleeping, every rite and ritual performed
exactly as it should, the altar laid out carefully as with
brushes, combs, the little pots of artifice –
a mother teaches her child the ancient spells,
- only this roll-call is conjured up in dreaming
Amazon, Venezuela, Colombia, Ecuador, Peru.

The Juggler Tree

Hardware

You steer me past nails, shiny as bait, spiked brushes for chimneys
wood turning tools, tongued and grooved flooring –
towards shelved tins of magnolia
      – very popular, very neutral you say.
Magnolia creates an illusion of space I'm told, as if
Baronial acres were sealed under lids, and muted, you add
-like mufflers and blinkers, turning down
what might otherwise be amplified
      – or worse, turned on. You even suggest
I 'do' the whole house the same magnolia shade
presumably so, I can glide through the house
like a bewildered shell in a magnolia hell.

Mr Hardware Man, in this magnollia wilderness
you do not quench my thirst. You don't see
vermillion in my amber eyes,
that it's red I want, hot on the skin of my bedroom walls,
atomic orange - taking me off in the kitchen,
songs of wild watermelon dripped from the bathroom tap.
And, when the shades are low, though you wouldn't know,
Magenta is on my lips, a tinge of Mediterranean blue
lusting in the hollow of my throat.
So keep your job lot
your creamy ten per cent off -

I'll take my business elsewhere.

Seahorse Sky

Bones

'Does a dragon still sting from within a withered tree?'- Dogen

What I touch is a woman with sharp corners
daggers at shoulder blade, knives in her eyes,

scratching the sky with broken fingernails.
Who breathes after sundown in shallow places.

There is a twist to her mouth and a sting on her tongue,
she smells of bees yet should have been a spider.

What I touch shapes the hourglass of days chipped from bark,
brown Sundays, the suck of a voice drowning in outer space.

Whitebeam Prow

Spit and Clay

In times of drought plants drop their leaves
conserving water, even the honeysuckle -
such bell shaped beauty - is willing as a novice
shaves her hair to the bone, to shed all vanity.
Fallen leaves, the generous scattering of petals,
give rest and shelter to the soil
as a wattle made from earth and water
acts as preservation.

Shoulder to wheel, nose to grindstone,
swallows too follow nature's deciduous ways
build their nests from spit and clay.

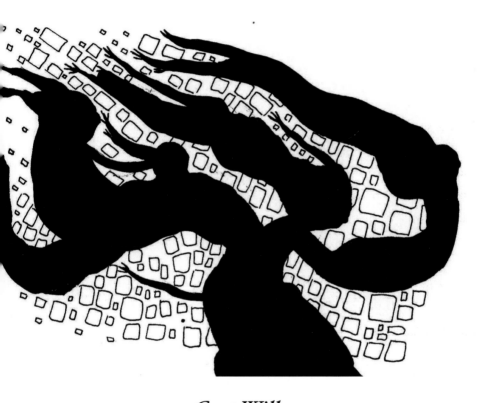

Goat Willow

Mulberry Dream

Stars stick like thistledown across a thumbnail sky
two daughters adrift in a world of juicy spring.

All night I search for mulberries
along the silken roads of Samarkand,

enough to glut the greedy worms. Spin two dresses.
Yet, all I can find is air, hard as frost, an aspen stump

gnarled between empty spaces and a rustling thirst
snagged on a blackthorn tree.

Rose Dragon

From Bone to Blossom

'What did the tree learn from the earth to be able to talk with the sky?'
-Pablo Neruda

Wisdom grows tall as trees of youth, there is much to make of the journey,
its push towards the light – darkness too. Without shade,
there would be no truths, no beauty borne by tender shoots or woods
to cross, clearings reached in spaces between earth and sky, tooth and claw.

Although, there's not much talk between Wild Cherry,
Noble Fir, trees, like humans, are wanting to know
who or what crunches through the leaves.

Contrary mates – one won't flower until September
the other quickening early spring,
leaves appearing only to be dropped again,
like a discarded lover, its woodland neighbour
growing cones, upright pillars. Edible
but bitter fruits of one, scattered
by birds, tangerine scented needles
piercing sharp as winter's bending bough.
Reminding us
how small we really are, spindling back to earth
like falling stars.
What then can be whispered to the skies?

Skyloom

Juniper Journey

I turn my back on bitter streets that taste of dust.

Rooftops lean together, silvering leaves spray houses
blushed by splashes of circumstance.
A thunk of cricket bat dazzles the droning bee
nets are down in tennis courts.

Iron gates, hazy with heat, swing open,
a pool of thirst licks lemon ice-cream
brought by Italians when they came here.
This earth is catkin green, pale yellow
flavours outhouses, illuminates fenced-in gardens.
Smells of smoke and steam
settle on branches, rise again like walkers on stilts
dappling dusk of late summer.

The world around me is tall and straight
undersides downy, cats eyes bright on leaf spine,
no sound of weeping, no sharp prick of needles.

Pages turn in blue silks of sleep
release the scents I pressed there.

Saturnalia

Soot *(For John)*

We should be drinking tea, reading newspapers,
shuffling our daughters from their beds. Instead,
masked and gloved, our furniture shrouded
in dustsheets, glass and mirrors covered,
our Sunday morning transforms to mourning room.

My role is this: deliver on cue each spiky rod,
keep down the mess – as all good wives should.
You my husband of so many winters passed
disappear to shoulder line up the tunnelling gateway
such caution - Hades himself might pull you up!

But you come back again – even Elysian Fields
could not tempt you from me now – none the worse,
except for charcoal speckles in your greying hair,
brimming shades of how it used to be.

Each time the rod goes up you give an extra heave,
Sisyphus rolling the stone so steep this chimney
climbing. Smells of smoke bring fires we burned
into lengthening evenings. The rods too
grow longer, divining their way to the top
shooting out like a hornbeam's domed crown.

(ii)

How many times you might, I wonder, have cheated death?
slipped away in sleep? As the sun too,
swerving on midnight bends, goes down, rises again.
This last push sheens your forehead –

you are no longer the boy in bare feet at Muckross shore
pulling on the tug of war rope – in another life.

A blizzard of soot floods our grate. Abundant sands,
like seeds carried by birds,
grow the toughest timber. Above our masks, eyes meet -
such pleased surprise we see –

as when our first born came shooting down
the birth canal, or, having flocked in rhythmic patterns,
we settle again on roosting branches,
shake our feathers clean.

The City of Love

(at The Lamberti Clock Tower, Verona)

At this stage of the coming up or going down
there's a flight of stairs and a sharp turn. No way
to manage but on foot. At the base of these steps,

like a climber without a Sherpa, sits a man
braced in heavy callipers.
His window gives postcard glimpses only,

the gods deal an extra blow
stranding him in this amphitheatre
while sparrows line the rooftops.

The elevator opens its doors, two men step out,
solid as oak or the stone walls in Galway,
sizing up what must − and will be done.

Hands interlock, form a sturdy chair,
taking the stairwell angle surely as a gondolier
the narrowest canal in the old city.

Birch Blossom

Timber

Blackthorn winters are covered in white
flamboyance blossoms on the blackthorn tree.
Veils of weather tangled in bustles, full length
coverings, crown to root.
Miss Havisham in mourning for summer
yet butterflies and birds find shelter.
Sloe too sour to eat is perfect
for the sipping days of youth.

Timber harvest is a bountiful one.
As chair is to rest,
bed is to rise and buck of passion,

walking stick to bone.

Surge

To celebrate my magenta coming of age

Arrive no later than half past three,
taste the scent of begonia spilling lazy
on the window sill, still as a Picasso.

All hazy left and plump bird shape
I stare down the hours on the hot clock of noon.

Shadow melts down the ledge,
wakes the sleeping cat
who stretches and lets out her claws
as if unlacing tight pinching whalebones.

Make a soft click with the latch
so I know it's you come
to fill this magenta coming of age space
with lighter shades of love and grace.